AWES
ANIMAL
STORIES

FOR 8 YEAR OLD KIDS

Book illustrations and cover design by Davor Ratkovic

Contents

An Impossible Journey

Have you ever been lost? It's pretty scary when you can't find your mom or dad. They probably found you pretty quickly, and then you felt good again. Being with our family makes us feel happy and safe.

Bobbie was a bob-tailed little collie mix kind of dog. He lived with the Brazier family in Oregon in 1923. The family loved Bobbie very much. They loved him so much that they couldn't imagine leaving him when they took a long family road trip over the summer. They decided to bring Bobbie with them on the trip. Bobbie thought it was great being able to ride in the car with his family. He loved exploring new places and smelling all the new things.

The family was staying the night at a little town in Indiana. This is a long way from Oregon. That evening, Mr. Brazier decided to go fill up the family car with gas. Bobbie went with him. When Mr. Brazier went into the store to pay, some local dogs came and started barking. They scared Bobbie, and he ran away. The other dogs chased him. Mr. Brazier came out of the store to see Bobbie running away. He tried

to call him, but Bobbie was too scared.

Mr. Brazier wasn't worried yet. Bobbie was a tough and smart dog. He should be able to find his way back. A few hours went by, and Bobbie was still missing. The family decided to look for him. They drove around town honking the car horn. At home, Bobbie always ran to the car when he heard the horn. But today, Bobbie didn't show up.

The next day, Mr. Brazier placed an ad in the newspaper looking for their lost dog. The family stayed in that little town for three more weeks, searching for their missing pet. They couldn't ever find him. The family was so sad. They had to go back home without Bobbie. They left instructions in case Bobbie was found. They would pay to have him sent home. The Brazier family made it home to Oregon. Their hearts were sad. They missed Bobbie.

Six months passed. It was wintertime. On a cold, dreary day, one of the girls, Nova Brazier, was walking with her friend in town. A scruffy dog ran out of the woods. Nova stared at the dog.

"Bobbie?" she asked. The little dog wiggled with excitement.

He jumped into Nova's arms and licked her face. Bobbie had somehow found his way home!

Nova took Bobbie home. The rest of the Braziers were so happy to see him. They knew it was Bobbie because of his bobtail and three scars. Bobbie was very skinny, and he was wearing a collar the family hadn't seen before. But they were sure it was him!

Bobbie's feet were really sore, and he had blood on them. He looked like he had a hard journey. The family wondered, could Bobbie have walked all the way from Indiana? That was a 2,800-mile trip! Poor Bobbie sure was tired. He didn't do anything but eat and sleep for three whole days.

Bobbie's story was shared in the local newspaper. Other newspapers shared the story too. People contacted the Brazier family. Some people had seen Bobbie on his travels. People along his journey had helped him. They had given him food and a place to sleep. All the people that helped Bobbie said he seemed eager to get on his way. It seemed like Bobbie had somewhere to go. He did! Bobbie wanted to be back with his family.

The family was able to trace most of Bobbie's long journey home. He seemed to follow the path they took. This led them to think Bobbie was following their scent. Bobbie traveled through plains, deserts, and even the Rocky Mountains.

Bobbie became a bit of a hero. He received a crazy amount of fan mail. He got to be the guest of honor at special events. He was even given a special large dog house. Best of all, Bobbie got to be back with the people he loved. Dogs are such wonderful, loyal friends!

Elephant Hero

Amber Owen was eight years old. She and her family were on vacation in Thailand. Amber liked playing on the beach. She liked exploring the beautiful land. She liked swimming in the sea. But her favorite part of the vacation was the elephants!

Every day, elephant trainers would bring their elephants to the beach. They would give rides to the children. They would let the elephants splash and play in the waves with children on their backs. It didn't take long before Amber had a special elephant friend. Ning Nong was a four-year-old elephant. Amber would bring him a banana every morning. She only wanted to ride Ning Nong. She would ride him every day on the beach and into the water.

After breakfast one morning, Amber ran ahead of her parents to the beach. She had a banana and was going to see Ning Nong. The elephant trainer helped her get on Ning Nong. Amber tried to ride the elephant out into the waves. Ning Nong did not want to go! She kept turning and heading back up the beach far from the shore. Even the trainer was having trouble controlling where Ning Nong was going.

The people on the beach didn't know it yet, but there was a huge natural disaster happening out at sea. A natural disaster is a sudden, terrible event that occurs in nature. There was a huge earthquake way out in the middle of the ocean. This earthquake formed a giant wave in the ocean. As it traveled toward land, the wave got bigger and faster. In some places, it was 100 feet tall. It traveled at 500 miles per hour. This is known as a tsunami. It is a huge, deadly wave.

The earthquake and the tsunami would cause damage in fourteen different countries. It was a huge event. Many people died. As Amber and Ning Nong were on the beach that morning, the people didn't know what was happening out at sea. But Ning Nong seemed to know. That's why she was acting so strange. She wanted to get to a safe place away from the beach and the giant wave.

As the wave got closer, the water from the beach pulled further in toward the ocean. This is a sign that a huge wave is going to hit. The people on the beach didn't know this. Many people came to the beach to see it. That's when the huge wave hit. Ning Nong was already running for safety. He stood strong against the swirling water. He kept Amber and the elephant trainer safe. Thanks to Ning Nong's instincts and quick thinking, Amber survived.

Amber's mother found her away from the beach, in a safe

space all thanks to Ning Nong. Many people died from this natural disaster. Thanks to a very smart elephant, Amber was just fine. Animals have smart instincts when it comes to storms and natural events. It's probably a good idea to listen

to what they are trying to tell us sometimes! Do you think this story will help convince your parents to get you a pet elephant?

The Incredible, Unsinkable Sam

Do cats really have nine lives?
Probably not. That's just a
way of saying cats are tough
animals. This is the story of one
tough cat, who survived a war
and three sinking ships!

At the beginning of World
War II, a little black and white

cat was put on a German ship. Many ships had cats living on them. The cats would help kill the mice. The mice could make a lot of trouble on a ship. They could eat wires, ropes, and important maps. The cats had a big job.

For a few months, the cat lived on this big boat out at sea. Then one day, the ship was attacked. It began to sink into the ocean. Not many people would survive this shipwreck.

Later that same day, another ship was passing near the wreck. The crew of the new ship saw something amazing. A little black and white cat was floating on a piece of wood. It was all by itself in the big ocean. The crew called, "Oscar, Oscar!" which means "Man overboard!" The crew was able to rescue the little cat. They brought him onto their ship. They decided to name him Oscar.

Oscar led a good life for about six months. But then, oh no! A torpedo hit the ship where Oscar lived. This ship began to sink, too. Fires started in some of the engine rooms. It was crazy as the sailors tried to get off the ship. Luckily, a sailor grabbed Oscar. He was put into a small raft. He was taken safely to shore.

Most cats would not want to go back out on a boat. But this cat was different. He was now known as "Unsinkable Sam." Sam went back out on a boat with another crew. Then it happened again. You guessed it...this ship was attacked too. It also began to sink!

Sam was picked up out of the water by one of the crew members. He was said to be angry but unharmed. This would be the last sea adventure for Sam. He ended up being sent to live at a home for retired sailors. He lived there, keeping the sailors company for the rest of his life. I wonder if any of the other sailors had also survived three separate ship attacks like Sam?

Stop Monkeying Around!

Going to the zoo is a fun
adventure. You get to see new
animals and learn about how
they live. In the 1930s, zoos
were still pretty new to America.
Many people had never seen the

types of animals that lived in zoos.

Frank Buck was a smart man. He liked animals and he liked to make money. Frank went on a trip to Brazil. He brought home several exotic birds from his trip. Frank was amazed. Rich people wanted to buy these birds for lots of money. This made Frank think. He knew he could travel and get more exotic animals. He could let people pay him to meet his wild animals.

Frank started collecting animals from other countries. He got tigers, leopards, monkeys, birds, and snakes. He would ride in the steamships with the animals when they traveled back to America. He did this to be sure the animals were safe. Sometimes he would sell the animals to other people or zoos. He kept some of the animals for himself.

At the Chicago World's Fair, Frank set up a display of some of his animals. People loved being able to meet these animals they had never seen before. The display was very popular. When the fair was over, Frank moved all of his animals to some land in New York. This became known as Frank Buck's Jungle Camp.

People loved visiting Frank's Jungle Camp. They could see so many new animals. Sometimes they would get to see brand new baby animals. The newspaper would come and take pictures when Frank got new animals or if a new baby was born.

One day the newspaper had to report on some not so good news. Frank's monkeys escaped from the zoo!

It was just like any other day at the zoo. One of the zoo workers went to clean the monkey cage. He set up a board over the long moat so he could get across. He got to work, cleaning and scrubbing. All of a sudden, he looked up. He had forgotten to remove the board across the moat. The monkeys had found it. They were running across and escaping!

The worker jumped into action. He told the other zoo workers. They tried to round up the loose monkeys. It was no use. They could only capture two monkeys. The rest took off out of the zoo. There were now 175 monkeys on the loose on Long Island, New York!

The police were called. They weren't very good at catching monkeys either. They only captured two more monkeys. At 4 pm, an express train was heading down the tracks. It had to come to a sudden halt. Fifty monkeys were climbing all over the tracks! They were hooting, howling, and having a wild time. The train conductor had never seen this. He had read about it happening in other countries. He was able to clear the tracks in just five minutes. The train was back on its way, but the monkeys were still loose.

As nighttime approached, thirty monkeys got sleepy and headed back to the zoo. So many monkeys were still missing. The police and zoo workers had to notify the local people. They didn't want the people to wake up with monkeys on their roofs! Would you like to wake up to find a monkey on top of your house? People were promised a cash reward or free zoo tickets if they could help catch the monkeys.

Over the next few days, most of the monkeys were captured and returned to the zoo. However, reports don't mention that ALL the monkeys were returned. This means that for a while, there were still some wild monkeys living it up in New York. What kind of fun would you have if you were to find a loose monkey?

These Rats Are Heroes

When you think of an animal that saves lives, you probably think of a dog. Dogs have been trained to find lost people. They work with soldiers to keep people safe. But there is another smaller animal that is also working to save lives. Guess what animal it is? This might surprise you. It's the rat!

A man named Bart heard about a problem in Africa. Some bad people had set up landmines. A landmine is like a tiny underground bomb. Nobody can see them. When someone steps on it, it explodes. People can get very hurt.

Bart thought this was terrible and very dangerous. He wanted to help. Police were trying to find these landmines, but it was tricky work. The chemicals used to make the landmines had a powerful smell. The smell could be detected by dogs. But it was dangerous work for dogs, too. Dogs were big enough that they could set off a landmine. This would make it explode. The police needed something even smaller.

Bart liked solving problems. He liked helping people. Bart had a pet rat as a kid. He remembered how smart the rat was. His rat loved people. Rats have really good noses. Bart put together a team. They got to work training rats.

It turns out, training rats was pretty easy. They used giant African pouch rats. There were a lot of them in the area. They have strong noses. The rats were trained to work with police

and soldiers. The police let the
rats out in the area they are
searching for landmines. The

rats are small enough that they can move around safely. They sniff for the tiny bombs. If they smell one underground, they scratch and dig at the area. This tells the police that there is a landmine there. The police and soldiers can then work safely. They know where the landmine is. They can get in and take it apart so it doesn't explode.

What does the rat get for doing a good job? A treat! Most rats love peanut butter and mashed bananas.

Rats started being used to find landmines in 2007. These trained rats have helped find over 56,000 landmines since then. This means they have saved thousands and thousands of people from getting hurt. Not one rat has ever been hurt while hunting for the landmines. So the next time someone says they think rats are gross, remember these life-saving rats in Africa!

Pickles the Soccer Dog

Dogs can use their noses to help humans in many amazing ways. Some dogs help police by sniffing for bombs and bad guys. Some dogs help in hospitals by sniffing for the scent of certain diseases. Dogs can use their noses to help find people who are lost. This is the story of how Pickles used his nose to find an unexpected lost treasure.

In 1966, England was very excited to host the soccer World Cup. This was a big event! The best soccer teams in the world would all compete to see who was the very best. The winner would take home the prize of the Jules Rimet Trophy. This was a fancy silver trophy insured for $30,000.

Before the World Cup games even began, the trophy was taken to England. It was set on display so soccer fans could go admire it. It had guards

that watched it all the time.
So imagine the surprise when
the trophy went missing! The
guards had only been gone for a
little while, but someone came
and stole the trophy. The people
of England were shocked. Who
would do such a thing? Where
was the trophy?

The police began to
investigate, but they didn't
have any good leads. The
next day, the president of the
soccer association received a
mysterious package. Inside
the package was the velvet
lining for the trophy. There was
also a ransom note. The note

demanded $15,000, or the thief would melt the trophy. Yikes!

The president of the soccer association and the police got to work. They created a bag full of fake money to trick the thieves. They dropped off the bag of money and waited. They caught the thief. But it turns out that he wasn't the trophy thief after all! He was just a dishonest guy who was trying to get money. He did not have the trophy.

The police were back where they started with no ideas on where to find the trophy. The people of England were so sad. Who would take the Jules Rimet trophy? Would they find it in time for the World Cup?

A few days later, David Corbett took his dog Pickles for a walk. Pickles was a black-and-white border collie. He was four years old. David took him for walks every day. On this day, Pickles got very excited. He pulled David through the yard. He was sniffing like crazy. He ran to a bush and started sniffing under it. David looked to see what was there. It was a package, wrapped in newspaper. It was pretty heavy. He unwrapped the package and couldn't believe it. It was the

Jules Rimet trophy! Pickles had found the stolen trophy.

The police came and confirmed that it was the real trophy. The trophy was given back to the soccer association just in time for the World Cup to start. At first, the police thought maybe David was the thief. But he had an alibi. That meant he could prove he wasn't anywhere near the robbery when it happened. The police never found the trophy thief, but they were very glad to have it back.

England ended up winning the World Cup that year. David got to go to a fancy dinner when the team won. He was given a reward for helping to recover the trophy. He used the reward money to help buy a house. The house had a nice yard for Pickles. Pickles was famous in England. He got to be on TV and star in some movies.

Pickles was just an ordinary dog. He didn't have any special police dog training. Pickles's story shows us that it doesn't always take any special training or skills to do the right thing. Sometimes, anyone can be a hero.

The Oldest Animal in the World

Do you think your parents are old? What about your grandparents? They've been alive a long time. They've probably gotten to see all kinds of cool stuff. But even your grandparents haven't been around as long as Jonathan the Tortoise. That's because Jonathan is 190 years old!

As I write this, Jonathan is the oldest animal alive. Can you imagine blowing out 190 candles on your birthday cake? Jonathan has been around for a long time. Vets and researchers have studied him. They aren't sure when he was born. He was brought to an island called St. Helena Island in 1882. He was given as a gift to Sir William Grey-Wilson. Sir William became the governor of St. Helena Island. Then Jonathan got to move to the fancy governor's mansion, called Plantation House.

Jonathan loved Plantation House. Sir William decided that Jonathan should live there his whole life. He still lives there today. Jonathan gets to wander around the gardens of Plantation House. He greets guests and tourists who come to see him. Since he is 190 years old, Jonathan isn't as spry as he used to be. He is blind and he has lost his sense of smell. He doesn't let that stop him from living life to its fullest. Jonathan enjoys grazing on grass, sunbathing, sleeping, and eating. What do you think a tortoise likes to eat? Jonathan's favorites are bananas, carrots, cabbage, and apples. He lives at Plantation House with three other tortoise friends. Their names are Emma, Fred, and David.

The cool thing about being alive for such a long time is witnessing how many things have changed. Jonathan has lived at Plantation House with thirty-one different governors. He has been alive for forty United States Presidents. Jonathan sailed to the island on a ship. Now we have cars, airplanes, and even rockets to help us travel. The world has changed a lot in 190 years. Humans have explored

and discovered new things.
If tortoises could talk, I'll bet
Jonathan would have some cool
stories to tell!

How long can a tortoise live?
Good question! A tortoise in the
wild usually lives for 80-150
years. How has Jonathan been
alive for so long? Jonathan lives

in captivity, meaning he lives
in a protected space. Jonathan
and his friends at Plantation
House don't have to worry about
predators attacking them. They
don't have to hunt for food or
fresh water. They get to live the
good life.

The oldest recorded animal
to ever live was another tortoise
named Adwaita. She lived at a
zoo in India and died in 2006.
Vets think Adwaita was 250
years old when she died.

Tortoises are not known
for being fast. In fact, they
are pretty slow. Their average
walking speed is a quarter mile

per hour. I think Jonathan and other tortoises are proving that with life, slow and steady wins the race.

Presidential Pets

If you became the United States president, you'd want to bring your pet with you to live in the White House, right? Other presidents felt the same way. Many animals have lived as pets in the White House.

What has been the most popular pet in the White House? If you guessed the dog, you're right! Thirty of the past forty-five presidents have had dogs as their pet. Other popular White House pets have been cats, birds, and guinea pigs. There have also been some crazy animals that have lived in the White House. Let's learn about some of these animals that called the White House home.

In 1825, President John Quincy Adams hosted a special guest from France. When the guest arrived, he had a gift for the president. It was an alligator! Back then, exotic animals were considered very special gifts. President Adams decided that the alligator could live in the East Room of the White House. This room had its own bathtub. A bathtub seemed

like the perfect place to keep an alligator.

President Martin Van Buren also received an exciting gift when he was the president. A Sultan gave him two tiger cubs! President Van Buren wanted to let the tiger cubs grow up living in the White House. Congress didn't think this was a good idea. They decided it was best to let the tigers live in the zoo. This was probably a good idea. I'm not sure that tigers make good pets.

Calvin Coolidge was president in 1926. That year, the states had a contest. Each state sent in different foods hoping to win the honor of being chosen for the president's Thanksgiving meal. Someone in Mississippi sent in a raccoon! The president was not eager to try eating a raccoon. Instead, he and his wife decided to keep the raccoon as a pet. They named her Rebecca. She got to live in the White House and eat fancy foods. Her favorites were shrimp, persimmons, and eggs. For Christmas, Rebecca received a pretty collar that said White House Raccoon. Rebecca would sometimes make trouble for the workers in the White House. She would open cabinets, unscrew lightbulbs, and dig in the plants. What a funny pet!

Other animals didn't get to live inside the White House, but they did get to live on the lawn. One president had a flock of sheep to help keep the yard trimmed. For many years, every president had at least one horse or pony that lived at the White House. This was when horses were used as transportation. When cars were invented, not as many presidents kept their horses. John F. Kennedy had several ponies for his children. Their pony, Macaroni, liked to have his photo taken. Teddy Roosevelt also had ponies for his children. One day, his sons even snuck their pony into the elevator and up to the second floor!

It's fun to learn about all the different animals that have lived in the White House. Even famous presidents like to have the friendship of their pets. What kind of pets would you have if you lived in the White House?

The Unstoppable Eagle Huntress

Aisholpan Nurgaiv is a thirteen-year-old girl who lives with her family in the country of Mongolia. Aisholpan does things that other girls her age do. She goes to school, helps out in her home, and likes to play with her friends. But Aisholpan has a pet that is a little different from most girls her age. Aisholpan has an eagle!

Aisholpan's family is part of the Kazakh people. They are nomads, which means they move around to different homes. They raise goats and cattle, and they are skilled hunters who hunt for meat and trade furs. The Kazakh people have a special tradition: they train golden eagles to help them hunt. The eagle and the handler have a special bond. When Kazakh boys are about 13 years old, they can begin to train and hunt with an eagle. They learn from their fathers and other men in the tribe.

Aisholpan helped take care of her father's eagle. She loved learning about the bird and seemed to have a gift for handling her father's eagle. Aisholpan really wanted to be able to train and hunt with her own eagle. However, Aisholpan faced a challenge – she was a girl. In Kazakh culture, girls were not allowed to train and hunt with golden eagles. For over 2,000 years, only men and boys had been allowed to be hunters.

Aisholpan's father didn't agree with this rule. He thought

Aisholpan should be able to hunt too, so he started to teach her. He was a very skilled eagle hunter and helped her learn many skills. Aisholpan had to work hard. When it was time for Aisholpan to select her eagle, she had to get it from the nest. The eagles are taken as baby

birds, raised, and trained by their human handlers.

Aisholpan named her eagle White Wings, and the eagle lives in the house with her family to help them bond. Aisholpan has to know the different moods of her eagle, which helps them have successful hunts.

When it is time to hunt, Aisholpan rides out on her pony with White Wings sitting on her arm. She finds a spot with a good view and then waits until she sees a rabbit or a fox in the distance. She releases White Wings to go hunt it. Aisholpan can't make White Wings hunt, but their bond and training make the bird want to hunt for her.

The Kazakh people have a special festival called the Golden Eagle Festival where about forty men and boys gather to show off their eagles and hunting skills. In 2016, Aisholpan became the first girl to compete in the Golden Eagle Festival. At first, some people didn't want a girl to compete, but they could see the strong bond Aisholpan had with White Wings and how hard the bird worked for her. Aisholpan and White Wings put in their best performance and won the hearts of many people. Incredibly, they also won the whole festival! They beat some of the best eagle trainers in Mongolia because they shared such a strong bond.

Aisholpan loves working with eagles and enjoys taking care of them. She hopes other girls in Mongolia will decide to hunt with golden eagles. She wants to encourage other girls and kids her age to bond with these cool animals.

Six More Weeks of Winter

Do you like watching the news on Groundhog Day? If the groundhog sees his shadow and goes back into his hole, you get six more weeks of winter. If he doesn't see his shadow, then it means spring is here!

The star of Groundhog Day is Punxsutawney Phil. Phil lives in Gobbler's Knob, a park in Punxsutawney, Pennsylvania. Phil is a groundhog. These are small rodent animals that like to burrow in the ground. They eat mostly grasses and berries. In the winter, groundhogs hibernate. This means they dig a deep burrow and sleep from October to March. When they do this, their heart rate slows way down. They only take one breath every 6 minutes.

The first Groundhog Day celebration happened in 1886. This was just a small party for the people of the little town. In

1993, a movie came out that made the town famous. The movie was called Groundhog Day. Suddenly, everyone knew about the town and its special tradition! Now, every year between ten and twenty thousand people visit the

town for the Groundhog Day celebration.

On the day of the event, people wake up at 3am. Wow, that's early! They head over to Gobbler's Knob, near Phil's burrow. There is a stage. There is a special group of people called the Inner Circle. They wear tuxedos and top hats. They help with the tasks that need to take place. Two scrolls have been prepared. One says spring is here. The other says six more weeks of winter. The president of the Inner Circle will "talk" to Phil in a special language. He will share what Phil says about winter and spring.

When the sun starts to come up, Phil will leave his burrow. He will come onto the stage and "talk" with the president. Everyone will wait! Will it be six more weeks of cold? Will it be spring? The President will share Phil's guess. Everyone will cheer either way. Then all the people head back into town. There will be a big festival with food, games and lots of fun.

Phil probably goes back to bed. Most groundhogs are not really done hibernating on February 2nd. During the year, Phil lives with his wife, Phyllis. They live in a small zoo where they have a cozy burrow. Tourists can come visit this famous groundhog. Most groundhogs only live about 6 years. The legend of Groundhog Day says that Phil is over 136 years old! They say Phil drinks a magic potion every year that helps him live forever. That sounds a little fishy to me.

How often is Phil right with his winter or spring guess? Phil has only guessed springtime about 20 times. He usually says it will be 6 more weeks of winter. Phil guesses right about 40 percent of the time. Groundhog Day is mostly just a fun way to celebrate an old tradition. Even if Phil guesses wrong, it is fun to know so much about Groundhog Day. You may even want to visit and see for yourself.

Hollywood is Cat Crazy

Every year, people move to Hollywood hoping to become famous. The city of Hollywood has grown bigger and bigger. Buildings and houses pushed into the wilderness as the city grew. When this happened, the wild animals moved away. They wanted to be able to hide in the forests and didn't want people to see them.

Somehow, in the busy town of Hollywood, a new cat arrived. This cat became pretty famous. He wasn't a movie star. In fact, he didn't even like people to see him at all. That's because he was a mountain lion! That's right. In the middle of Hollywood, a mountain lion roamed around loose for at least ten years.

His name was P-22. He set up his home right near the famous Hollywood sign. Instead of being scared of him, people respected him. So how did he move to Hollywood? That's a tale that could probably be a movie. P-22 was born in a mountain range 50 miles away from Hollywood. There were about 100 other mountain lions living in that area. And how did P-22 get his name? Forest rangers were studying these mountain lions. The "P" stands for puma, and he was the 22nd puma recorded in that area.

P-22 must have felt the need for an adventure. He set off on a trip and traveled the fifty miles toward the city. He even crossed two huge highways without being seen. Then, P-22 settled

into a big local park. He decided
it would be a good place to live,
right under the Hollywood sign.

The park ran a study of
the animals and birds that
lived there. Imagine their
surprise when they discovered

a mountain lion! People could have been scared, as mountain lions are big, fierce wild animals. But the local people decided that he deserved to live there, too. P-22 mostly kept to himself. He didn't like to be seen. He hunted at night, hid, and slept during the day. P-22 died in 2022, after ten years of living near the movie stars in Hollywood.

Having a mountain lion move into the city reminded people that animals need places to live, too. We need to protect their land and food. This is called conservation. P-22 helped people learn about conservation.

The people of Hollywood even decided to build a big bridge, called a land bridge, to help wild animals move safely across the busy highways. Having a local mountain lion helped people become more aware of the wild animals around them. It's important to remember that animals need places to live, food, and water. Even though cities are growing, it is important to remember to take care of the earth and the plants and animals that live here, too. What would you think about a mountain lion living in your town?

Cuddles the Guide Horse

You probably already know what a guide dog does. That is a dog that has special training. They can help a blind person move and walk around town without bumping into things. They help keep them safe. Pretty cool!

What if I told you that horses were being trained the same way? No, not BIG horses but little, tiny horses called miniature horses. The people training them are finding out that these little horses make great guides for the blind. They are smart and easy to train. They bond with their humans. And they are also incredibly cute!

Janet and Don were horse lovers. They trained and rode horses all the time. Janet started to notice how some horses were good at reading traffic. They knew not to cross the street if a car was coming. They could move around things that blocked their way. Janet started to wonder if a horse could be trained as a guide horse. She got to work on her own miniature horse at home. Her name was Twinkie.

Twinkie was easy to train. She was small enough that she could ride in a car. Janet and Don took her to new places. They practiced letting her be a guide. Mostly, she did a good job. But one time, she did try to steal a candy bar off the shelf at the store. Silly Twinkie!

A man named Dan heard about the seeing eye horse.

He knew he wanted one. Dan had slowly lost his vision. He had trouble getting around and doing normal things. He needed help. He didn't want a guide dog. His pet dog had just recently died. It made Dan so sad. He didn't want to go through that again. Horses can live much longer than dogs. This seemed like a great idea to Dan. He decided to give it a try.

Janet selected a horse named Cuddles. She trained Cuddles to be Dan's guide horse. She worked with Cuddles for a long time. Finally, it was time for Dan to meet Cuddles. He flew on an airplane to meet her. Janet,

Dan, and Cuddles trained together for many weeks. When they were ready, Dan took Cuddles home. Dan had a barn and field all ready for Cuddles.

With Cuddles as his guide, Dan can have a more normal life. She can tell him where to go. She can warn him if he needs to step up or down. She keeps him safe in traffic. Dan lives in a small town. Everyone knows and likes Cuddles. Dan says he is lucky to have Cuddles. They make a great team.

The miniature horses that get chosen to be guide horses have to be easy to train. They usually aren't very big. They only weigh as much as a big dog. They can ride in a car. They can go inside houses and buildings. The horses are even potty-trained! They tap

their hoof on the door when they need to go outside. They wear special sneakers on their hooves so they don't slip. When the guide horses aren't working, they live in a barn and have a field to eat grass. That is the time for them to rest and relax.

While most blind people would choose to get a guide dog, a guide horse is a neat idea, too. A guide horse will live longer than a guide dog. They are also a good choice for someone who is allergic to dogs. And there's just not much that is cuter than a miniature horse. They're simply adorable.

A Beary Hairy Actor

Which movie star is nine
and a half feet tall, weighs
1,500 pounds, and was one
of the biggest movie stars in
Hollywood? If you guessed Bart
the Bear, you'd be right!

Bart was an Alaskan Kodiak
bear. He was born in a zoo.

He was just a tiny five-pound fluffball! As a baby, he was adopted by Doug and Lynne Seus. They are animal trainers, and they love working with bears. They started training Bart. They trained him to follow commands. Bart was easy to be around. Lynne and Doug started to think that Bart could be used in movies. They trained him to roar on command. He could stand up on his back feet and look very scary.

Bart's first movie was set in the wild west, and it was about cowboys and Native Americans. Bart did a really good job. He got asked to be in other movies.

Bart was in eleven movies. He got to act right next to some of the most famous movie stars of the time. The other actors all had great respect for Bart. They admired how he could turn on his bear charm and his roar when needed.

Then Bart got the leading role! He was going to be the star of his first movie. The movie was called The Bear. It was about an adult bear. Bart makes friends with an orphaned cub. The two team up to beat some hunters. The movie was a big success. Everyone thought Bart should win an Academy Award. That's a fancy award for actors and movies.

At that time, animals weren't allowed to win. Luckily, Bart probably didn't really care.

Years later, Bart did get the chance to attend the Academy Awards show. He was a presenter, which meant that he handed a special card to an actor. Can you imagine having a HUGE bear on the stage with so many people all around? Bart did a good job, and everyone was happy to see him honored.

Lynne and Doug wanted to use Bart to help other bears. They wanted to teach bear safety. They wanted to teach people about the bear's habitat. It is important to protect the land that bears call home. Thanks to Bart and his trainers, many more people know about bears. People know how to act around bears and that it is important to keep bears and their habitat safe.

Penguin's Got A Brand New Pair of Shoes?

Luca is a young African penguin. He lives in a zoo in California. He is four years old. Most penguins love to climb rocks and swim. They like to play with other penguins. Luca wished he could do that, too.

But Luca has a problem with his foot. It makes it hard for him to run and play.

This is known as bumblefoot. Some bad germs got into Luca's foot. This caused a painful area on the foot. It even hurts when he walks around. If the sores don't get treated, they can make Luca really sick. The vets at the zoo do a good job. But sometimes, Luca's foot still gets very sore. This makes him sad and not want to play with his friends.

Penguins are social birds. They live in large groups with other penguins. It is important for them to be able to swim and

play to be healthy. The African
penguin is actually endangered.
This means there are not many
of this kind of penguin left in
the world. It is important to
keep them healthy and safe. The
workers and vets thought it was
important to keep Luca happy.
They decided to see if there was
anything else they could do to
help Luca with his sore foot.

A company named Thera-
Paw thought that they might be
able to help. Thera-Paw makes
special boots for animals. The
boots help the animals be more
comfortable and active. They
help prevent slipping and help
with sore paws. But could

they help a penguin? They had never made special boots for a penguin before.

The people at Thera-Paw wanted to help. They came up with a special design just for Luca. The boots were very soft. They have Velcro straps to help get them on and off easily. They made them black, just like Luca's feet! It was important that the boots blend in with Luca. Sometimes

animals peck at things that are different colors.

To create the boots, they needed to get the imprint of Luca's feet. This is like when you trace your hand. They made Luca walk across an area full of sand. His footprints helped the people at Thera-Paw design the boots.

The boots fit Luca well. Suddenly, Luca was able to be active again. His feet didn't hurt. He started swimming and climbing on rocks. He made some new friends and even set up a new nest. Before the boots, Luca's sore feet made him shy.

Now he feels good and is leading a happy, active life!

The vets and zoo workers wanted the best for Luca. They cared for him and wanted him to have a great life. They wanted him to be happy. Thanks to these people and the people at Thera-Paw, a special penguin has boots to keep him feeling good. That is cute to think about!

Parrot to the Rescue!

Have you ever heard a parrot talk? Parrots are known as birds that can talk or mimic sounds they hear. Mimic means to repeat something. Some parrots can speak up to a thousand different words. They are very smart birds.

Willie was a quaker parrot. He lived with his owner, Meagan. They also lived with Meagan's friend Samantha and her daughter, Hannah. Quaker parrots are birds that like to talk. They usually speak around 50-60 words very well. Willie liked to talk and make funny noises. His favorite thing to say was, "Silly Willie!" He could sing some songs and imitate the sound of a human giving a kiss. He could also bark like a dog, meow like a cat, and cluck like a chicken!

Several mornings a week, Meagan would babysit 2-year-old Hannah. One morning, Meagan was making breakfast for Hannah. She was fixing a Pop-tart. Hannah was watching TV in the other room. Meagan left the Pop-tart to cool on the table. While it cooled, Meagan went to the bathroom.

Meagan had only been gone for a minute. Suddenly, Willie began to scream and flap his wings. He was squawking and being so loud. Then Meagan heard what the bird was saying. He kept repeating, "Mama! Baby! Mama! Baby!"

Meagan rushed into the kitchen to see what was wrong. She found Hannah. She was choking on the Pop-tart. Hannah had climbed up on the table and taken too big of a

bite. Now she couldn't breathe. Meagan had to act fast. She dislodged the food that was stuck in Hannah's throat. She made sure she could breathe. She calmed the little girl down.

As soon as Hannah was calm, Willie became calm, too. He had been very excited when Hannah was choking. When Hannah's mom got home, she couldn't believe it. She was so thankful for Willie. She thanked Meagan for helping Hannah. Meagan gave all the credit to Willie. His loud squawking got her to move fast.

Willie had never used the words "mama" and "baby"

together. And he hasn't used them together since that day. It seemed like Willie knew just what words were needed to save Hannah's life. What a smart bird!

YOUR REVIEW

What if I told you that just one minute out of your life could bring joy and jubilation to everyone working at a kids book company?

What am I yapping about? I'm talking about leaving this book a review.

I promise you, we take them **VERY seriously**. Don't believe me?

Each time right after someone just like you leaves this book a review, a little siren goes off right here in our office. And when it does we all pump our fists with pure happiness.

A disco ball pops out of the ceiling, flashing lights come on... it's party time!

Roger, our marketing guy, always and I mean always, starts flossing like a crazy person and keeps it up for awhile. He's pretty good at it. (It's a silly dance he does, not cleaning his teeth)

Sarah, our office manager, runs outside and gives everyone up and down the street high fives. She's always out of breath when she comes back but it's worth it!

Our editors work up in the loft and when they hear the review siren, they all jump into the swirly slide and ride down into a giant pit of marshmallows where they roll around and make marshmallow angels. (It's a little weird, but tons of fun)

So reviews are a pretty big deal for us.

It means a lot and helps others just like you who also might enjoy this book, find it too.

You're the best!

Printed in Great Britain
by Amazon